A CHILD'S WARTIME YEAR IN THE BLACKDOWNS

A MEMOIR

by

Stella Palmer (née Slade)

*To Jan,
With best wishes,
Stella*

Dedication

This memoir is dedicated to the memory of the Podbery family who showed such kindness to me in those wartime days.

Acknowledgements

I would like to thank my husband and many friends who have encouraged and helped me in the production of this memoir. Thanks are also due to the current owners of Higher Beetham farm for permission to photograph the building.

A CHILD'S WARTIME YEAR

IN THE BLACKDOWNS

Index

Dedication		3
Acknowledgements		5
Index		7
Author's Note		9
One	A background of war	11
Two	Life on the farm	15
Three	Life at school	29
Four	Time off	35
Author's Postscript		45
Appendix	Farmhouse survey	51

Author's Note

The characters in this account are real and not fictitious. I would like to emphasise that the material is a child's recollections of a particular period which have been set down with an adult perspective and some later research. Any misconceptions or imperfections must be ascribed to the passage of time.

One

A background of war

By 1940 the war was making life difficult and dangerous as night time air attacks increased. Living as we did in Surrey, ten miles south of London, bombs were often offloaded as German planes returned home and it was decided to send my mother, sister, aged three, and myself, aged seven, to Yeovil in Somerset to stay with my maternal grandparents, leaving my father at home to continue his work for the local council. We spent a great deal of time during the war going back and forth to Somerset, where I managed to attend infant, junior and senior schools in the ensuing period.

My grandmother's house overlooked the town, surrounded by green hills, and it was also a place beloved of bombers which attacked the Westland Aircraft works from time to time. It was one of my chief delights to watch from an upstairs window when the siren went and see the ring of barrage balloons rising all round the town – until I was removed to a safer place. I walked to school and enjoyed living with Gran, often visiting other relations in the town. Sometimes, when there seemed to be a lull in enemy activity my mother and sister Miriam would return home, leaving me with Gran. Life continued thus for some time until my grandfather died in August 1940. Looking back now I can see how difficult it must have been for Gran, who was forced to let the downstairs part of the house, leaving only two rooms for us all upstairs, plus the bathroom. It was then that someone had the brilliant idea of sending me to live on a farm near Chard owned by one of Gran's friends.

This was the beginning of a wonderful year for me, a year that has stayed with me for the rest of my life. I now know that May 1940 saw Winston Churchill's first days as Prime Minister, the defeat and fall of France and the evacuation from Dunkirk. There followed eight months in which Great Britain stood alone - the only European power left to carry on the struggle; eight months in which the German fleet tried hard to snap the lifelines which brought willing aid to the island, particularly from the United States; eight months in which the Luftwaffe tried and failed to drive the RAF from the skies; eight months in which Mr Churchill led a grim and resolute people in resistance to every challenge.

I was fortunate not to be exported on a train, my gasmask hanging round my neck, to arrive at the home of a totally unknown family, with whom I would have to live. I was unaware of the full horror of war, knowing of course of Hitler, bombs, gasmasks and evacuation, but sheltered from it by the love and care of a new family and a series of new and exciting experiences.

Two

Life on the farm

Beetham farm (above) was large after the flat in Yeovil, with no running water except for a cold tap in the scullery. There was an old iron pump outside the front door, pictured below, being operated by the author. I believe that the water from the pump spring supplied the scullery tap. It certainly tasted very good.

There were no mod cons at all - no gas, no electricity, no telephone - certainly no television, and outside, at the end of the walled vegetable garden, was the loo. The latter was fascinating. The small hut contained a long bench, where one sat over what appeared to be a bottomless pit and toilet paper was provided by pages of disused bus timetables stuck on a prong. We went to bed with a candle, and a hot water bottle when the weather required one. The bedroom contained a double bed with feather mattress, chest of drawers, wardrobe and washstand. On the stand there was a large china basin with matching jug, containing cold water, also a soap dish. The obligatory chamber pot was under the bed. The best bedroom had a rather splendid wooden commode. There were other bedrooms upstairs, the disused ones providing storage for trays of russet apples and onions, which were kept under the beds.

The main room of the farm was the stone-flagged kitchen with large open fireplace where water was constantly heated in large black kettles on the big wood fire, and sometimes a delicious stew simmered in a huge black witch's cauldron. The room was lit by a paraffin lamp in the evenings. Standing in the fireplace beside the fire, the sky was visible up above, past the sides of bacon hung in the chimney on hooks. A large wooden settle stood at right angles to the fire, mostly used by some of the many cats who lived there. A long flagged passage led to the back recesses of the house, where the dairy, scullery and some windowless rooms were to be found. The dairy usually contained large zinc troughs where pork was salted. Most people managed to butcher and consume their own pork and bacon, probably illegally in wartime, but none the less delicious. A small parlour lay to the other side of the kitchen where there was a piano and lots of sheet music of current hits like "Run Rabbit Run" and "The White Cliffs of Dover" which I was able to pick out with one finger. The farm building was the semi-detached half of a much larger building and subsequent research has revealed that it dated back to 1600. A plan and report on the farm can be found in the Appendix. Our half of the farmhouse was in fact the working half and therefore lacked the reception rooms presumably to be seen next door. We had no contact at all with the household in the rest of the building and, as with so many of these old farmhouses, the flagged entrance passage would originally have divided the kitchen department from the rest of the house where, surely there must have been a large staircase; ours was a small staircase accessed by a latched door from the kitchen.

My new family consisted of Tommy Podbery, the farmer, his wife Gracie and their daughter Maggie who was in her early twenties. The snapshot shows Tommy and Gracie, with me, held by Perce, the labourer, accompanied by his dog.

There was another daughter called Mary, but she was nanny to a family at some distance away, where she lived in. Tommy had been born in Devon and brought up in a farming family on the high Blackdowns beyond Churchstanton. He had a hoarse, rasping voice, strong Devon accent, almost unintelligible to me, and twinkly blue eyes. He sat at table wielding a lethal-looking two-pronged fork, and matching knife, impaling pieces of meat and hard fried bacon fat on his fork and enjoying both food and strong tea equally. He once showed me how to trap rabbits by placing a noose in the grass under a hedge or similar likely pathway for a rabbit, which resulted in the garrotting of the rabbit and a good dinner for the family. He also used gin traps, but these did not kill the animal and other unfortunates were often trapped by them. Gracie hailed from a Quantock family. She was a buxom, cheery soul with rosy cheeks and was very kind. She had married Tommy in Taunton many years previously and they had lived at Beetham many years by wartime. They welcomed me warmly and made me feel as though I belonged there, and not like an official "evacuee", children at that time being shipped off by train to unknown families all over the country.

At first it seemed like a holiday, since my mother and sister were there. We went for walks, helped with the harvest, picked mushrooms in the top field and enjoyed farm life. My mother particularly enjoyed gathering up the hens' eggs in the afternoon, a job which always seemed to fall to the lot of the farmer's wife. After settling me in and arranging for my school they left for Gran's in Yeovil, leaving me in my new home, but returning for the occasional visit. My father visited a few times and there is a snapshot below of all my family in a haycart, drawn by Flower.

My position in the family was soon established and it seemed to be that of young daughter. I shared Mag's feather bed, and became her shadow, trotting round after her like a small dog as she went about her work on the farm. The pictures below show us sitting on a felled tree trunk.

Mag's job of assisting her father on the farm was endless, and she surely did the work of several landgirls. Mag rose early and after a quick wash at the washstand in the bedroom she went down to the kitchen to make tea, if her father had not already done so. I followed shortly afterwards and we enjoyed our tea accompanied by hardbakes – these being very tough and long bread rolls which we dipped in the hot tea. Then on with the wellies and out to milk the cows, which Tommy had usually fetched and we found them waiting in their stalls. I think there were at least twenty of them. Unfortunately I was no good at all at milking, since my small hands were not strong enough to grasp the teats firmly and no milk was produced, in spite of many tries on a very patient cow, who must have thought it extremely strange. So on fine days I stood and talked to Mag while she milked. To do this she sat on a three legged stool and wore an old hat which protected her head as she rested it on the cow's side. In preparation for the milking it was necessary to wipe the cows' teats and also their tails, since they were often extremely filthy and liable to smack the milker in the face and possibly dirty the fresh milk in the pail. The new milk was carried to an outbuilding where it was strained into the cooler and then into the churn. The full churns were dragged to the end of the drive to await collection by a lorry from something called the Milk Marketing Board, I believe. When my mother visited the farm her favourite treat was a glass of fresh, warm milk, straight from the cow.

Mrs Podbery (whom I called Pod) had cooked the breakfast by the time we got in from milking, and we enjoyed eggs and bacon in the big, warm kitchen, where I sat at the end of the long table in the window seat. Whatever else happened on the farm the cows and their milking needs came first, so I got used to that quite quickly. After school I would go with Mag to fetch the cows from whatever field they happened to be in that day and they would return to their own places in the cowshed where it was my job to chain them up ready for the evening's milking. They were Devon Shorthorns and all had names like Daisy and Buttercup, my favourite being rather a scraggy cow called Jane. Cows were no respecters of persons and one soon learned to keep an eye open for possible dangers when walking along the cowshed behind them, as they relieved themselves copiously without any warning. I enjoyed another job which was trying to wean the calves from their mothers. This was done by encouraging the calf to drink from a bucket of milk by letting him or her suck milk from your fingers held under the surface of the milk. This made me laugh as their rough tongues tickled my fingers. After a day or two the calves grew weary of the false teats and managed to drink properly from the bucket of milk. The job I liked best was feeding the bull. I was sometimes sent to the cowshed, where the huge bull was chained up in his own private stall, and, approaching from the front, I was able to place large helpings of cabbage in his manger. Whether this was a safe thing to do, completely alone, I do not know, but the bull enjoyed the visits, and so did I!

Other events in the farm calendar, such as harvest were busy times. We all went out to help or hinder making sheaves from the stooks of corn left by the combine-harvester - a ferocious machine loaned to smaller farmers - and fine weather was essential during the period of hire. As the cutting started round the perimeter of the field and went round, approaching the centre of the field in ever-decreasing circles, the harvesters would form a large circle, waiting for the rabbits to emerge from the middle. This was fun until one came straight like an arrow in my direction and disappeared between my legs. I was teased about this for a long time afterwards since I was supposed to have caught it. Usually the crop harvested was wheat or barley, but the worst one was beans. Beans were left until brown and scratchy. I could not pick them up and was happy not to be there for their particular harvest. During my excursions into the fields for haymaking and harvest I always wore a poke bonnet with a little frill round the back of the neck to prevent sunburn. I have since seen such bonnets worn by farm girls in Victorian photographs.

As it was a mixed farm, cows predominated among the animals, but there were also a few pigs and sheep. When walking through the fields with Mag it was quite usual for her to be visited by one of the sheep. Alex, short for Alexandra the princess, no doubt, had been hand reared by Mag as a lamb, and every time Mag set foot in her field she would raise her head and set off towards Mag for a quick cuddle. She would also come when called by name. I must not forget to mention the two heavy horses, one a bay and the larger, called Flower, black with a white nose. They are shown on the following snap, the author and her sister on Flower, father holding the reins and mother beside him.

The horses did a lot of work ploughing, haymaking, sowing etc, pulling various implements and carts. The carts were interesting as they had high sloping sides and usually the name of the owner or previous owner painted on the sides. One may be seen in the snap on page 21, with my family aboard.

One breakfast time in spring, I was told that one of the cows had calved, in case I wanted to see the baby before going to school. I rushed out to the cowshed but found nothing unusual – then realised it was April 1st, and this was Tommy's idea of a joke. I was very cross with him for some time after that. He was a terrible tease.

There were a lot of farm buildings, including stabling for the carthorses, room for pigs and calves and a large barn full of ancient machinery such as a cider press and some old ploughs. Beyond the buildings was a large mound, partially covered in grass and I loved running along the top of it. This I was told was a Neolithic barrow, much sought after by archaeologists. Tommy had no time for such people "I baint 'aving they buggers 'ere digging up my varm" he would say. Whether or not excavations have taken place since, I cannot say.

Three

Life at School

During term time I did not share in the morning milking, but got myself ready for the day at school. Pod provided me with a lunch box which contained my sandwiches and a small flask of Ovaltine. I presume I carried this in some sort of satchel. I do not remember carrying my gas mask while in the country, the likelihood of a gas attack seeming extremely remote. I often wore my wellingtons to school as the lanes were muddy and the boots with big socks were warmer in winter. Also a large Shetland scarf was wrapped round me on top of my overcoat. The distance to walk was about a mile and there was no traffic, the lanes being just wide enough for one car or horse and cart. The hedges on either side were quite high and full of wild flowers in spring and summer. For the most part the walk to school was uneventful, but two particular things remain in my mind. One was a plague of large black stag beetles which covered the lane from side to side one hot day. I was forced to climb up the hedge and edge my way along above them until it was safe to come down. The other was the sheer volume of snow in winter. The drifts covered the lane and rose half way up the hedges, making walking quite hard work. The ensuing thaw filled the ditches with gurgling water and made the already muddy road muddier than ever, but then with wellington boots, who cared?

The school was in a small hamlet and consisted of one large room in which the sole teacher functioned. She was called Mrs Hodges (this is as well as I can remember her name) and she was a small, dark-haired lady who maintained order and imparted knowledge single handed. She was generally well-liked and I joined the class ranging in age from five to fourteen. The children were all local and seemed not to mind the stranger amongst them. There was a large coke-fired stove in the room surrounded by an iron railing on which we hung our dripping clothes on wet days. We sat round the stove in the winter to eat our lunch. On one occasion my flask must have broken inside and when I opened it a fountain of Ovaltine gushed out all over me and the schoolroom. This was most embarrassing. On fine days we played in the playground, mostly at hopscotch, which took various forms and needed a particular sort of flat sided pebble to move smoothly over the ground and arrive on the right square. Much time was spent in looking for the right pebbles for this game. I enjoyed going to this school, so different from the larger school I was used to. The time passed there quite pleasantly and I remember going on a treasure hunt in the lanes, looking for various things specified by Mrs Hodges. The periwinkles were in flower at the time and I can picture them now. We seemed to have frequent spelling tests and my frustration was great when I could not get the words right. One particular word was "gnarled", which I spelt as "knarled", knowing there was something odd about it, but getting the first letter wrong!

There was an older boy in the class who was quite friendly. One day he handed me a small folded note, written in pencil. I put this in my pocket to read on the way home and discovered it was my first love letter. I did not know what to do with this, but feeling that it should be kept a secret I decided to hide it in a bird's nest I had spotted in the hedge in the lane near the farm. I left it there, deciding to look at it again another day. I was not particularly moved by Philip's declaration of love, and I think he produced another note in similar vein. This note also went into the bird's nest. Unfortunately Philip became ill with ringworm. I remember him sitting at the end of the schoolroom on his own with a large round red mark on his forehead, looking pale and watery-eyed. Was this something one caught from cows? I was absolutely amazed when I next looked into the nest to find no notes. Someone had stolen them I thought, but who? I vaguely remembered a rustling in the opposite hedge when I looked in the nest the first time. Then I remembered that there was a young man living at the farm opposite the nest who had learning difficulties, as they would describe it today, and was looked after by two spinster sisters, or possibly a mother and aunt. He must have seen me and taken the notes. I did not say anything as we had no particular contact with these neighbours and I still felt the notes should be kept a secret. And so it has remained until now.

There was another event concerning school, which caused a more serious problem. In the summer term a second school was opened in the church hall to house two teachers and the evacuee children who had been billeted locally. I was asked to find out if my parents wanted me to stay where I was or move to the other school. I do not remember being given a letter to take home, as such things did not exist. Of course I forgot to ask anyone, there was no telephone, and since I felt Pod was not my parent, did nothing about it. Of course the day dawned when I had to give an answer. "Who wants to move?" inquired Mrs Hodges. Thinking on my feet I put up my hand and knew at once that I had done the wrong thing. She appeared disappointed and said nothing, but I knew I had made the wrong decision. My childish reasoning was that I was more or less an official evacuee and perhaps should be considered as such by the school and take my chance with the London lot. And so I did.

I think there were only a few weeks left before the end of the summer term. I remember nothing regarding the teaching or the children except for one incident. We were larking about outside and one of the bigger girls picked me up bodily. She lifted me up and I cracked my head on the metal casement window of the village hall which was open above us. This hurt terribly and my head bled quite a bit. Divine retribution no doubt for deserting Mrs Hodges I thought, and decided it was all my own fault. Worse was to come. At the end of term my father came down from Surrey to visit his family and made a point of going to the village school to thank Mrs Hodges for all she had done for me during the year. The war was taking a slight turn for the better regarding air raids and it was decided that I would return to Yeovil to stay at Gran's with my mother and sister for the following term. I stood there in mute horror while he spoke to her – surely my treachery would now come to light. I looked desperately at Mrs Hodges, who spoke happily to my father, saying nice things about me and not a word about the rival school in the church hall. I then realised that she had known all along that I had not consulted any grown up about the move, and we parted with affection. The school is now (2012) a private residence but looks virtually the same and there is a picture of it below.

Four

Time off

On Friday evenings Mag and I would go to choir practice at the vicarage. This was quite an experience and taken by the vicar, Mr Doorbar. He possessed a splendid Oxford accent and always greeted Mag by "Ah, Meggie!" which meant that he was very pleased to see her. So he was, as she was the star soprano performer in the choir, which was small in number, and was accompanied by a lady organist on the organ, which was pumped by a lad. On one occasion I remember Mag sang **The Holy City** standing on the chancel steps and we were all very proud of her. It was a long walk to the village, in the opposite direction from my walk to school, and I think I was rather tired by the end of Friday. We saw a big glow in the sky when we returned one evening and it turned out that the Germans had decided to offload some bombs at Ilminster. Apart from this incident the war did not really affect me much in my rural retreat, though I am sure it affected the rest of the family. Petrol was hard to come by and meant that visits to market in Ilminster, Chard or Honiton were rare and a trip to Taunton best done on the bus. Not that the bus functioned every day and we had to walk to the village to find the bus. It was on one of these shopping visits that we went to the pictures and saw the film **The Great Dictator**. I preferred Chard or Honiton to Taunton as they both had channels of water running down their High Streets. I always enjoyed watching the auctioning of the cattle, sheep and pigs on market days.

When the weather was wet my usual indoor pursuit was reading, which I loved. I also spent some time picking out tunes on the piano in the parlour from Mag's sheet music. When sitting on the settle with the cats I used to attack the fleas which inhabited the ears of the oldest cat, firmly attached, they had to be pulled off and I would throw them into the fire, where they hissed on contact with the flames. This latter occupation was not encouraged, but I thought I was helping the cat.

Saturday was not my favourite day because although I had time off school, Mag also had time off and often spent the afternoon looking after Jill (seen above), a teenager from the village, and they would go riding together. This left me at home with Pod, and the dreadful experience of having my hair washed. I had a lot of hair, put into short plaits, and although the washing part was bearable the drying was not and the combing out of tangled hair a very painful thing indeed – no conditioner in those days! Pod did her best, and I was always clean and tidy. We enjoyed a weekly bath in a zinc bath filled from the black kettles on the fire, the bathroom being what Mag termed the 'dark hole', one of the windowless rooms at the back of the house. We all contrived to be bathed at the weekend, particularly so in view of church on Sunday, when we would set off for church in the village, there and back on foot of course, unless there were a few extra drops of petrol. The one occasion when the car was put to great use was for the village dance. I am pleased to say that I always went to the village dance since the family could not leave me at home on my own. Pod always helped with the refreshments, Mr Pod wanted to visit his pals at the pub, and Mag wanted to meet the young men from other villages. Sometimes her sister Mary turned up for the dance and we all had a great time getting ready. I must have looked a bit odd in my best knitted pink dress and black woollen stockings, but no one ever complained about my youth and I really enjoyed dancing. My favourite was the Paul Jones, in which the girls walked round in a circle one way and the men in an inner circle going in the opposite direction, everyone stopping when the music did in front of the eventual partner. I expect some of the men were disappointed to get me instead of a beautiful girl but that thought never occurred to me at the time.

It was at these dances that Mag met the young man from Devon who was to become her husband. He was a farmer's son called Jack, was tall and gentle with lovely brown eyes. He came from Stockland in Devon. He and I got on very well and later he came to visit Mag at the farm, eventually becoming engaged to her. Some time later I was invited to visit a snowy Somerset to be a bridesmaid at their wedding. I shared this privilege with Mag's sister Mary and her friend Jill. The best man was called Nip and he ended up in the forces. War shortages managed to deprive me of a suitable bridesmaid's dress but I was arrayed in a friend's white velvet confirmation dress with Juliet cap and best black school shoes. Perfect! I was to return to Devon fifty years later to join the other bridesmaids at the golden wedding celebration for Mag and Jack.

Mary, Nip, Jill and me

The wedding group - Mr Podbery is to be seen in the background, right hand side

Pod was the secretary of the Women's Institute and during holiday times I would accompany her to the meetings in the village. She had a big round hand and filled many exercise books with accounts of the doings of the WI. I enjoyed **Jerusalem** at the beginning of the meeting and also the tea and cake later on. The President was an important lady called Mrs George who lived at the big house in the village, and in the summer we once had a fete in her garden. I remember little except some large hats.

Food at the farm was delicious to my rationed tastebuds. Pod cooked well and a range of new meals enthralled me such as rabbit pie or stew – I liked to be given the head so I could eat the brains, a great delicacy. Mr Pod was a frequent producer of rabbits, which he shot or trapped on his way round the farm. I often helped Pod to skin the rabbits - a simple job, if you were strong enough to pull hard on the skin. There was also ham and bacon, plenty of fresh eggs and on occasion, delectable trifle. Trifle was served in a gigantic glass bowl, the top covered generously in scalded cream, which was better than clotted cream. Another of Pod's specialities was Welsh cakes, a sort of fruit scone fried in dripping. I think the fat content was quite high, but all the more tasty for that. In the dairy there were large zinc trays containing pork joints steeping in brine resulting in excellent salt pork, and sometimes there was brawn also.

One great meal was the harvest supper. Here all the workers came into the kitchen and sat round the long table, enjoying Pod's lovely food such as cold ham and pork, cheese, tomatoes and trifle. The Harvest Mug full of cider was passed round and I joined in drinking from it for Mr Pod had made the cider himself and I was not usually allowed to have it. "God Speed the Plough" was written on the side together with a poem, the words of which are long forgotten. Christmas dinner must also have been a great experience, but I have little recollection of it. I still treasure my present, the Bible given me by Mag and Mary, now rather worn, with Mag's inscription inside.

For relaxation there were sometimes walks in the lanes, to visit other farms and friends of the family. Pod's sister lived in another ancient farm building and I soon knew my way round that farm as well. Picking mushrooms in the fields was fun, also blackberrying, wild strawberry picking and gathering hazelnuts. We once had a great picnic at the top of Castle Neroche, which had a magnificent view of the rest of Somerset. We had to be careful that time not to disturb an adder which was sleeping in the bracken.

Returning home to Surrey after my time in the Blackdowns I was met by my father at Waterloo station, having made the journey care of the guard. "Did you have a good time?" he said. "Oooh-aarrh" was the reply, and that just about sums it up.

Author's **Postscript**

At the end of the war I spent a holiday with Pod and Mr Pod, who had by then moved farms to the next village. I was pleased to have the chance to explore another farm, and also went to stay for two weeks with Mag, who now lived with her husband on the family farm in Stockland, Devon. She was also the proud possessor of Tommy, her first child, and I was able to hold him and play with him, a fact he finds possibly embarrassing now he is in charge of the same farm. But I have the snapshot to prove it!

The author with Tommy

In 1965 my father died. Pod wrote a wonderful letter of condolence to my mother, which is shown below.

Keats Cottage
Bishopswood
Chard.

May 20th

Dear Rosie & All.

It was kind of Thirza to write but oh we are so sorry to hear the sad news. Altho' I know you would rather he was taken than stay & suffer. He will be sadly missed not only by his dear ones but also by his very large circle of friends of which we hope we may be counted. It was always such a treat when you came to see us. I cannot believe was that it was little more than a year ago when we had such a lovely afternoon together & you both seemed so well. God give you strength and the comfort of his Holy Spirit to help you. I am sure you are far from well yourself. You know that if at any time we can do anything for you. it would be such a pleasure. I am so glad you have Missy & her husband & darling little Catherine with you & apparently will be with you. & I am sure willbe

a great comfort to you. Our thoughts will be with you tomorrow. With loving thoughts to you which include Stella Michael & the children
Ever your old & loving friends
Gracie & Tommy

P.S. I am sure Mag & Mary will wish to associate themselves with what I have written

Appendix

The following pages are reproduced with the permission of the Somerset Archives and Local Studies Service, the document number being DD/V/CHR/3/9.

Somerset Vernacular Building Research Group

Affiliated to the Somerset Archaeological and Natural History Society
and to The Vernacular Architecture Group

S V B R G

SURVEY
with the permission of
Mr I. & Mrs H. Cumming
and Ms M. Herring

HIGHER BEETHAM
FARM & HIGHER
BEETHAM
FARMHOUSE
Buckland St Mary
JMcC, LH, PP-T,
AR, JC, JD
August 2006

NOTE: For the purpose of this Report the two houses will be dealt with as one.

LOCATION
National Grid ref. ST 278 121. Buckland St Mary C.P. (until boundary changes in 1982 it had been part of Combe St Nicholas C.P.), South Somerset D.C. area. The house is part of an isolated farmstead (divided into two in 1804 see History Notes below) some of the farm-buildings have been converted to independent dwellings in recent years.

LISTING
Not listed by the Secretary of State for the Environment as being of special architectural or historic interest.

PLAN.
Two-storey. Four rooms and cross-passage in-line with additions on the east and west sides.

EXTERIOR
Walls of Unit 1 average 65cm thick whereas the walls of Unit 2 average 56cm thick all are of local rubble stone (part rendered). The gables have Ham stone stepped copings. The stack at the north end is of Ham stone ashlar with water-tabling but the others are brick.
Windows are casement type – formerly of timber - many have been replaced in recent years, those in the northern half on the east front have been fitted with re-constituted concrete mullions and surrounds.
The roof is clad with double-roman clay tiles.

INTERIOR
Fireplaces:
F3 is an inglenook having a bead moulded timber bressumer; an opening in the right-hand jamb was probably a tunnel communicating with a curing chamber which has subsequently gone but the curved wall confirms that it existed. The void on the left-hand side is likely to have contained a baking oven earlier.
F4 and the associated stack was probably inserted at some time after the house was divided into two (ca.1804).
F1 was the original Hall fireplace which has a timber lintel with a 7cm deep flat chamfer and a masons mitre at either end – as the mitres are not aligned with the present jambs it is probable that the jambs have been re-built. An oven opens from the left-hand jamb.
F2 is blocked and built-up, it has a timber lintel with camber and 7cm deep chamfer.

Door openings:
A number of earlier openings have been blocked.

Stairs:
The present two flights of timber stairs were inserted after the division in 1804. Whereas the stairs originally would have been in the traditional position at ST? - adjoining the Hall stack - the curvature of the walls in the opening ST?? may indicate that there could have been another flight!

Roof structure:
Comprises tie and collar trusses, the one purlin each side is jointed to the principals with tusk-tenons there is a through ridge-piece with planted yoke piece. The ties and yoke are nailed to the principals.

INTERPRETATION & COMMENT

Datable evidence is sparce but the plan-form and the variations in wall thicknesses and the non-alignment of the back walls (S) indicate that there were a number of periods of build.

Phase I
The details of fireplaces F1 and F2 suggest a ca.1600 date of build. The house then comprised the Hall (H) and Inner Room (IR) with entry at D1 in what was then the gable-end. The Inner Room may not have been heated at that time – the stack and fireplace being added a little later.

Phase II
The low end (that is, the Cross-passage 'XP', Kitchen 'K' and Parlour 'P') is unusually long and may have been a new addition or a re-building (and lengthening) of some earlier structure. Based on the details of the bressummer to fireplace F3 it is of an 18th century date of build.
As the roof structure is of this period and is uniform over both Units 1 and 2 it is likely that it was renewed at this time – the pitch and water-tabling suggests that it was probably then still thatched.

Phase III
After the division of the house in 1804, the new party-wall was inserted, the room 'P' was formed and the fireplace F4 and stack were inserted as well as stairs ST3.
The entire roof was probably re-clad with clay tiles late in the 19th century and it is in this period that the two service rooms 'S' -- probably as dairy and cheese rooms - were added..

Phase IV
Various alterations occurred during the 20th century, including the removal of the curing chamber, the blocking of the W-end of the Cross-passage – and a window inserted, fireplaces F2 was blocked and the curing chamber 'CC' was removed and probably the oven removed. Some doorways were blocked and other openings created.
New windows were inserted in the N-front of Unit 2.

HISTORY NOTES
At the time of the Tithe Map c.1839 the two holdings were each about 100 acres.
A schedule of owners and occupiers is attached and it is noted that the property had been leased from the Dean & Chapter of Wells Cathedral until Unit 1 was bought in 1891 and Unit 2 in 1913 and the composition of the respective farmsteads was described at that time – a Block Plan (drg.no.2) shows some of the buildings which existed ca.1970 (per the present owner of Unit 1).

John Dallimore
August 2006

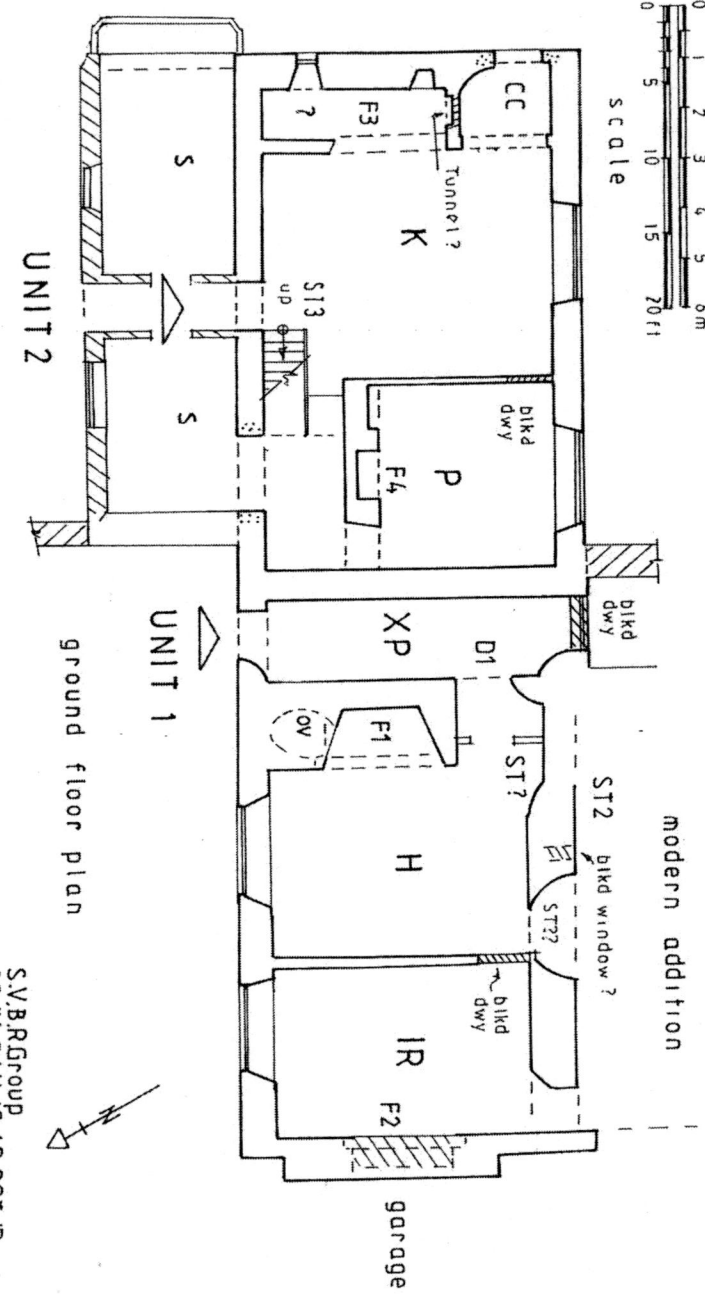

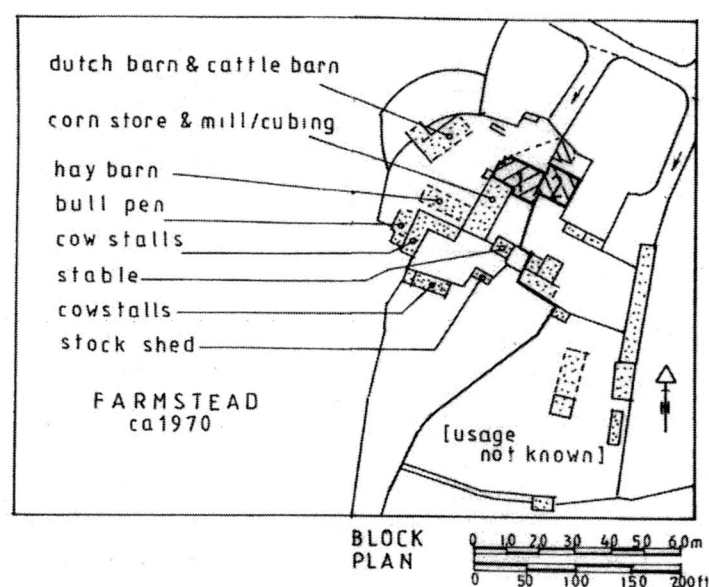

BLOCK PLAN

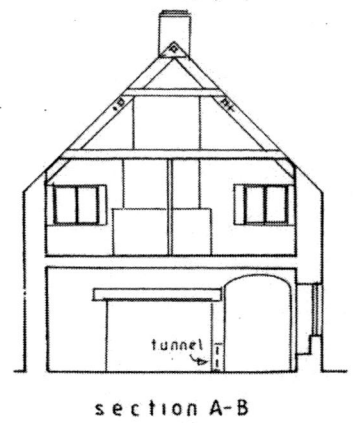

section A-B

drg. no. 2   S.V.B.R.Gp.